She is HOPE for Wildlife

The Story of Wildlife Rescuer
HOPE SWINIMER

Written by
Wanda Baxter

Illustrated by
Leah Boudreau

NIMBUS
PUBLISHING
NIMBUS.CA

Text copyright © Wanda Baxter, 2024
Artwork copyright © Leah Boudreau, 2024

All rights reserved. No part of this book may be reproduced, stored in a retrieval system or transmitted in any form or by any means without the prior written permission from the publisher, or, in the case of photocopying or other reprographic copying, permission from Access Copyright, 1 Yonge Street, Suite 1900, Toronto, Ontario M5E 1E5.

Nimbus Publishing Limited
3660 Strawberry Hill Street, Halifax, NS, B3K 5A9
(902) 455-4286 nimbus.ca

Printed and bound in Canada
NB1678

Editor: Penelope Jackson
Art direction: Whitney Moran & Heather Bryan
Design: Bee Stanton

Nimbus Publishing is based in Kjipuktuk, Mi'kma'ki, the traditional territory of the Mi'kmaq People.

Library and Archives Canada Cataloguing in Publication

Title: She is hope for wildlife : the story of wildlife rescuer Hope Swinimer / written by Wanda Baxter ; illustrated by Leah Boudreau.
Names: Baxter, Wanda, 1969- author. | Boudreau, Leah, illustrator.
Identifiers: Canadiana (print) 20240407474 | Canadiana (ebook) 20240409426 | ISBN 9781774713327 (softcover) | ISBN 9781774713334 (EPUB)
Subjects: LCSH: Swinimer, Hope—Juvenile literature. | LCSH: Wildlife rehabilitators—Nova Scotia—Biography—Juvenile literature. | LCGFT: Biographies. | LCGFT: Picture books.
Classification: LCC SF996.45 .B39 2024 | DDC j639.9092—dc23

Nimbus Publishing acknowledges the financial support for its publishing activities from the Government of Canada, the Canada Council for the Arts, and from the Province of Nova Scotia. We are pleased to work in partnership with the Province of Nova Scotia to develop and promote our creative industries for the benefit of all Nova Scotians.

For Hope Swinimer, real-life wildlife rescuer and founder of Hope for Wildlife. And for Maddy and Peter, Olive, James, Stevie, Nikki, Maya, Campbell, and Graceland.

In memory of Gretel the pine marten, and Reid Patterson.
Wanda Baxter

*For my family,
thank you for supporting me every step of the way.*
Leah Boudreau

She is Hope for Wildlife beautifully captures my childhood passion for nature and my journey to make my unique dreams come true. I hope this inspiring book encourages young readers to realize the impact they can have on the world around them by pursuing their vision, and persevering until they achieve those goals.
Hope Swinimer

Table of Contents

Prologue..................................... 1

Part 1: Growing Up in Argyle 2

Part 2: Learning from Wildlife.............. 10

Part 3: Building Hope for Wildlife 18

Epilogue: A Focus on Joy.................... 37

Hope's Timeline............................. 41

Sources 43

About Hope for Wildlife 43

About the Author and Illustrator 44

Prologue

The word *hope* means "to want something to happen, and believe that it will."

Hope Swinimer will live up to her name and grow up to rescue thousands and thousands of wild animals and birds. She will inspire people all around the world to care about wildlife, and support wildlife rescues. But first, she needs to find her way.

This is Hope's story—so far.

Part 1: Growing Up in Argyle

"Come and see, Hope!"

And Hope went running out to the garden out to where her mother was holding a field mouse gently in her hands.

Hope put her face down right in front of the mouse's face, and saw that it was scared.

"One of its legs is hurt, and it won't survive outside, but I knew you would want to see."

"It's all right, Shorty. I'll take care of you."

"You can't keep a mouse, Hope. That's not what people do," said her mother.

"You have to let me try!" said Hope, and her mother couldn't say no.

So Hope got a cage, and put some hay in one side so the mouse could make a nest.

"The other side is where it will eat and play, but it needs something to exercise on," Hope said to her brother Sidney, who liked to build things.

Sidney wanted to help, so he found an empty Graves apple juice can and turned it into a makeshift running wheel for Shorty.

"That's Hope's mouse running again," the neighbours would say, sitting on their decks in the evening, listening to the squeaking wheel and shaking their heads. They couldn't understand why Hope cared so much about a little mouse.

Hope couldn't understand why they didn't care about the little mouse like she did.

Hope grew up in Argyle, a small community by the sea on the southwest tip of Nova Scotia. She was the youngest and shyest of four children, two boys and two girls, and it was a free and happy life, growing up.

Her family lived in an old house with a view of the ocean, they had a big vegetable garden, and they were thankful for what they

had. While they didn't have much, they didn't know it—because no one else had much either.

Hope's best friend, Darlene, lived on her grandmother's farm next door. They'd signal over to each other when the tide was high, then they'd grab their bikes and pedal down to the wharf where they swam all day and played in the waves like seals.

There were horses and other animals on Darlene's grandmother's farm. And Hope had a favourite: a black-and-white paint horse called Firecracker. (She liked him the most because he had "spunk.")

"YeehaWWW!"

Hope was quiet and shy by nature, but she wasn't afraid.

She and Darlene rode the horses without a saddle, or bareback, when they were big enough to climb on. Riding bareback is hard because horses are slippery and round, so they fell off a lot.

"But we got right back on!"

When she wasn't riding bikes and horses with Darlene, Hope spent a lot of time outside on her own. She loved to learn about things by watching, quietly. She would sit for hours patiently observing the world, watching frogs and birds and squirrels and insects, and she'd make notes and drawings about what she saw.

One day at school, her teacher saw her sketching in her notebook.

"It looks like you're interested in nature and animals, Hope," her teacher said. "Have you thought about what you want to do when you finish high school?"

"I want to make a place where animals are free and safe to roam," said Hope, "and people and animals live without fear of each other."

"It's a beautiful dream," her teacher agreed.

Hope also dreamed of studying science or having her own farm someday, but it didn't seem possible. Hope's parents were a great influence on her. They were frugal and worked hard at their jobs, but university wasn't an option for most people back then, and as hard as Hope's parents worked, they weren't able to support her after high school.

Hope was good with numbers, and she thought if she could train to do something practical, like accounting, she could make enough money to save up and buy a farm someday. The problem was, to be an accountant you had to go to college, and she didn't have the money for that.

But Hope, being Hope, didn't give up.

There has to be a way, she thought.

And so…Hope figured out a way.

She picked strawberries and blueberries in the summer to sell by the roadside. Sometimes she would see a bear (or a few bears) up on the hill in the distance, eating berries in the sun. It made her happy to see they weren't afraid of her (and she wasn't afraid of them).

Hope sold health-care products door-to-door, too, riding around to people's houses on her bike. Hope was still very shy, but she was determined to save enough money to go to school. And finally, after a lot of berry picking and door-to-door sales, she did.

Part 2: Learning from Wildlife

Hope was only sixteen years old when she left Argyle to go to college to study accounting almost a four-hour drive away in Truro. She had never been so far from home, and they were hard times for Hope. She was lonely and far from everything she knew, and she had barely enough money to get by. Some people took advantage of how kind and trusting and young she was. Still, Hope refused to give up.

She worked part-time as a cleaner to pay her bills, she studied hard, and before long Hope had finished her courses and found a job as an accountant. She wasn't working with animals or nature like she'd dreamed, but she was finding her way—all on her own.

Hope's first job out of school was for a trucking company, and that's where she met Zorro the skunk! One of the truckers came into work one day, and said he'd picked up a skunk that had been hit by a car. He asked Hope if she knew what he should do.

Hope went out to his truck, took one look at the skunk, and named him on the spot. He would be the first of many skunks she'd name Zorro.

Hope took Zorro home. She set up a cage in the backyard, and then she had to teach herself how to take care of him. One of his eyes was injured and he had a broken leg. She got advice from vets and books because there was no one else she could learn from back then. His eye and leg eventually healed, but he couldn't see well enough to survive on his own. Zorro would never be able to be released back to the wild, so Hope got a permit to keep him.

After a while, even the neighbours who used to complain about the smell of skunk coming from Hope's yard started to like Zorro.

Once you get to know a skunk (and it doesn't spray anymore), it's hard not to like them. They have dark, expressive eyes, and long nails for digging in the dirt. They stomp their feet when they're scared, and they smack their lips when they're happy.

Zorro lived at Hope's until he was fourteen years old (a *really* long life for a skunk!).

"He was my guiding light," Hope says. "He's the one who showed me what I wanted to do."

After taking care of Zorro, Hope knew she wanted to work with animals all the time. She was already working part-time at the Dartmouth Veterinary Hospital on top of her accounting job, but she wanted to learn more about working with animals. She went back to school at night to learn how to manage animal hospitals. When she graduated as a Veterinary Practice Manager, it meant she could manage the vet clinic where she worked. It would turn out to be the perfect training for running a wildlife rescue.

One day at her new job as a vet manager, Hope's life changed forever. She was working at her desk when a woman arrived with an injured robin. Her cat had brought it in, still alive, and the woman wanted the vet to save it. Hope asked the vet if they could help.

"We can patch it up, Hope," said the vet, "but it will need to be fed and taken care of, and we can't do that here."

"If you tell me what to do medically, I'll take care of him myself at home," Hope replied. And that was the start of Hope working with vets to help rescue hurt wildlife.

Hope went back out to the people in the waiting room and asked if she could see the hurt robin. It was cuddled up on a bit of hay in the bottom of a shoebox.

Hope took Bobbi home and followed the vets' instructions. She'd learned his clavicle (or collarbone) was broken, and it would heal with time. Hope asked for advice any time she needed it from the vets, who knew how to treat pet birds. Mostly, she needed to keep him calm and try to keep him from flying.

"It's all right, Bobbi. We'll take care of you."

She fed Bobbi the food he needed (including worms from her garden and small bits of fruit), she made sure he was safe and warm, and she took care of him until he got better.

It took a lot of time and patience, but eventually he *did* get better!

Finally, when Bobbi was strong enough and able to fly, Hope took him back to where he was originally found to set him free. She put his box down on the ground, then opened the top and tipped it gently over. Bobbi took a few uncertain hops and looked around, and then he flew away.

After that first success with Bobbi the robin, Hope started learning everything she could about wildlife rehabilitation (which means taking care of sick or hurt animals until they can return to the wild). She read any book she could find, and she started training wherever she could. She went to the closest wildlife rehab, in New Brunswick, to learn. She went to a rehab for raptors (which are birds of prey, like eagles and hawks), and she went to Maine to get certified as a wildlife rehabilitator.

Hope worked hard to get certified, and soon she was ready

to rescue animals on her own. She needed a place where she could rehab animals and birds, so she bought a rickety old trailer and some land in Seaforth, near Halifax. Hope's father took one look at it and said he was worried she was wasting her time and money. But later, when he saw what she did to fix up the place and how well she worked with the animals, he was surprised.

Hope surprises a lot of people. They tell her things can't be done, and she proves them wrong over and over.

Word started to get around that a woman named Hope was rehabilitating hurt wildlife in Seaforth. And, as word continued to spread, more wildlife started to arrive.

Hope might come home to find a box of orphaned raccoons on her doorstep, or an otter in a bucket. Other times people would bring a fox—or a mink, or a bobcat, or a turtle, or an owl, or a hare—that had been hit by a car but wasn't dead.

People would arrive with a still-alive squirrel the cat had brought in, or a bird that flew into their window (because it couldn't see the glass).

And there were orphaned baby birds, too: blue jays and hummingbirds, owlets and waxwings, sparrows and swallows, goslings, ducklings, and baby loons, or "loonlets."

There wasn't anywhere else to take injured wildlife, so people took them to Hope. And Hope wanted to help them all.

Part 3: Building Hope for Wildlife

It wasn't long before Hope needed more room to house all the animals and birds people were bringing her. The neighbours started to complain about the noise and some were nervous about what she was doing. They didn't understand why she was keeping wild animals in her backyard. She needed a bigger property for her growing wildlife rescue. It was time to move *again*.

Hope didn't have much money, but she looked and looked until she found something she could afford: a drafty old farmhouse in Seaforth. Nestled on a hill by a lake—with forest all around, and a view of the ocean in the distance—it reminded her of Argyle. She felt like she was home.

The old farm was a perfect place for a wildlife rescue. Now she just needed a name.

That part was easy: it would be called Hope for Wildlife.

Hope got a call one day about two American pine marten pups. Their mother had died, and the orphans were left helpless. Hope agreed to take them in, and she named the pups Hansel and Gretel. Hope had never seen a pine marten before, but she was immediately taken by the reddish, weasel-like animals with cute faces.

Hansel and Gretel needed constant care. Hope fed them day and night from a bottle. Hansel had the same illness as his mother, and sadly he didn't survive. But Hope was able to save Gretel.

The government department in charge of wildlife heard about the rescued pine marten, and they arrived at Hope for Wildlife to take Gretel away. They told Hope that Gretel was an endangered species and it was illegal to keep her. They told Hope to release Gretel to them.

It made no sense to Hope. She had been asked to raise the orphans and she worked hard to save Gretel (and there are so few pine marten left!). She refused to let the government officers take her.

Luckily, a lawyer heard about what was happening and got in touch with Hope. They offered to help her fight to keep Gretel and go to court if they had to.

The story was picked up by the media and got international attention. People around the world started hearing about the wildlife rescuer named Hope who wasn't allowed to keep the endangered pine marten she'd saved—even though Gretel would die if she was set free. That didn't seem right to Hope, and it didn't seem right to a lot of people.

Eventually, after a *long* fight and a lot of public pressure, Hope was given permission to keep Gretel at Hope for Wildlife—as long as she would be used as an education animal. As it turned out, Gretel was an excellent teacher. Many people have learned about pine martens and the threats to the entire species because of her.

"Because of you, people will learn how awesome pine martens are."

For all the years she spent at Hope for Wildlife, Gretel was well loved and cared for, and she lived until she was seventeen years old (an *incredibly* long life for a pine marten).

Hope was on her own through all of this. She had a team of volunteers and staff to help her with the rescue, and she had the animals and Gretel for company, but at times it could get lonely.

Until love arrived, with the first fawn of spring.

A rugged-looking local fisherman named Reid arrived at Hope for Wildlife one day to donate some fish he'd caught. While he was there, he asked Hope if she'd go to dinner with him. She answered yes—on the spot!

The night of their first date, Hope was getting ready when she got a call about a wildlife emergency. A deer had been hit by a car, and a baby fawn was left without a mother. Hope called Reid and told him she had to cancel their date because an orphaned fawn was coming in. Hope thought that would be the end of Reid, but what he said next surprised her: he offered to come over and help her with the fawn, instead.

"Our first date was the twenty-seventh of May, just after the arrival of the first fawn of spring. That's when we celebrated our anniversary every year," says Hope.

Reid became Hope's right-hand man and partner, and he helped her build the rehab into what it is now.

He built a lot of the cages and enclosures at Hope for Wildlife over time. And, with his big fisherman's hands, he could hold four bottles at once to feed baby fawns.

Hope's fight to rehabilitate and keep Gretel got a *lot* of media attention. The story also got the attention of a local television show producer.

They arrived one day and asked Hope if she would be interested in doing a TV show about her work and the rehab.

She wasn't sure what to think. She was surprised, but intrigued. Hope didn't have time to spare, and she didn't think a TV show would help her help *wildlife*, which was all she cared about. But she didn't say no.

"We think a show could teach people to care about wildlife, like you do. And a lot of people would watch it."

"Let me sleep on it."

Everyone told Hope *not* to do the show. Her family and friends told her not to do it. Volunteers and staff told her not to do it. Even Reid didn't think she should do it.

Hope considered everyone's advice and opinions. She also thought about what a TV show could do.

She wanted more people to know and care about what happens to wildlife. She wanted to teach people how to live *with* wildlife, and how to avoid hurting wild creatures. She thought a TV show might help her do that. She also thought a TV show might help bring in donations—which the rehab badly needed. She had been running Hope for Wildlife with her own money, and the rehab needed all the donations she could get.

In the end, Hope went with her gut.

She took a leap of faith, and said yes to doing the show.

As it turned out, Hope's gut was right.

Hope for Wildlife TV turned out to be a huge success. It has been shown all over the world in over a hundred countries since first airing in 2009, and it continues to be well loved today.

The show was successful because people connect to Hope's warm personality and her genuine love for all creatures. The audience loves the caring, dedicated, and quirky volunteers and staff at Hope for Wildlife. They love the sometimes-funny wildlife rescues, the heartwarming releases, and the moments of joy and heartbreak that happen every day at Hope for Wildlife. The show is successful because it captures the real magic that happens there.

As *Hope for Wildlife TV* grew in popularity, Hope's prediction also came true: donations poured in from all over the world. With more donations, Hope and her growing team of volunteers and staff have been able to improve and grow Hope for Wildlife.

Here's an idea of how Hope for Wildlife has changed over time:

Reid helped to build a new **fly-way cage** for the large predator birds to practice flying and get stronger before they're released.

An **education centre** was built and then expanded on.

There is a new **recovery building** with individual rooms for long-term recovering animals.

Outdoor, habitat-like enclosures were built for long-term education animals like Freddie the fox, and others for bobcats, raccoons, and more.

Volunteers and interns built **gardens** (including a **rooftop garden** on the education centre, and a **pollinator garden** for butterflies and bees).

A **viewing tower** was built at the top of the hill for viewing the whole of the farm, the ocean in the distance.

Eventually a **marine centre** was built to rehab beavers, seals, and other animals that live in the water.

Rows of **solar panels** were added at the top of the hill to provide power to the rehab centre.

Walking trails were built and expanded on over time.

The **deer facility** was built (with stalls, like a horse barn), and a large deer enclosure was added, giving the older fawns more room to roam and graze.

Eventually, one huge donation enabled Hope and her team to build a new, **state-of-the-art nursery** for all the baby animals, called Fenton Farmhouse.

A **training/event building** was built behind the hospital building.

Hope's **old farmhouse** was torn down, finally, and she moved into the top-floor apartment of the new building.

In 2022 a **brand-new bird recovery facility** was built, and Hope for Wildlife acquired a grant to build ten new education exhibits.

Every year, Hope and her team host a huge open house, and anyone who wants to learn about rescuing wildlife (and meet Hope) is invited to come.

The morning of the open house, cars are lined up along both sides of the highway as far as you can see. Members of a motorcycle club help to direct cars, and a limousine picks people up from their cars if they park too far away to walk. Visitors bring presents and donations, and children give their saved-up birthday money to Hope—to help the animals. They wait in line to have their picture taken with her. She smiles her big, kind smile, and greets everyone with open arms.

There is live music playing, farm animals to meet and information booths to visit, tours of the rehab and the education centre. There are food and popcorn vendors, and someone selling baked goods. People climb the viewing tower to get a bird's-eye view of the whole farm.

The resident peacocks wander the grounds, their turquoise feathers trailing behind them. Ducks and geese wander the edge of the lake.

Seals bob and play in their pools at the top of the hill, bobcats stare down from high in the trees of their enclosure (you feel them before you see them), and the wildlife patients who need quiet to get better are kept in the hospital away from the crowd.

Hope is like a glowing presence at the centre of this fairy-tale world she's made.

When the big day is over and everyone is gone, Hope is still there working until dark, same as every day, cleaning up, feeding animals, and taking more wildlife calls.

Hope has overcome a lot of challenges since she started rehabilitating wildlife in 1995. But nothing makes Hope give up, or slow down, or stop dreaming of what more she can do.

"I could live two lifetimes and still not finish everything I want to accomplish," she says. "But the journey so far has been incredible, and more rewarding than I ever dreamed it would be."

Epilogue: A Focus on Joy

When fawns arrive at Hope for Wildlife in the spring and summer as orphans, they still have their spots on. By the fall, they are big enough to survive on their own.

In October of every year, the young deer are loaded onto a horse trailer, and are released in small herds back into the wild.

Releasing the deer in the fall is one of Hope's favourite things. It's what keeps her going: she focuses on what gives her joy.

"There's something magical about it," she says. "I haven't missed a deer release in all the years. I remember one year in particular: The snow was falling down beautifully, just floating down as the young deer were released. It was the most beautiful image you can imagine."

Hope's Timeline

1959	Hope is born
1977	Hope leaves Argyle for college in Truro
1995	First rehabilitated animal released back to the wild (robin brought to the vet)
1995	First wildlife rehab certification
1995	Rehab opens at Eastern Passage
1997	Hope receives Nova Scotia Wildlife Rehabilitation Permit and moves to Winnies Way in Seaforth
1998	First volunteer recruitment
2001	Rehab moves to the old farmhouse and Hope acquires more property in Seaforth
2002	First Open House day
2004	Hope meets "right-hand man," Reid Patterson
2006	Rescue officially named Hope for Wildlife
2006	First white-tailed deer rehab facility opens
2007	New nursery and hundred-foot flight cage built
2009	*Hope for Wildlife TV* starts filming
2011	Fenton Farmhouse rehab facility built
2015	Hope wins Courage to Give Back Award
2019	Hope awarded Honorary Doctor of Science from St. Mary's University
2023	Hope awarded the Order of Nova Scotia
2024	Eleventh season of *Hope for Wildlife TV* resumes filming (after Covid hiatus), to be released in 2025.

Over the years, Hope has helped to rescue more than 80,000 injured animals from 250 species. She has more than lived up to the meaning of her name.

Sources

She is Hope for Wildlife is based on a series of interviews carried out by the author with Hope Swinimer over the winter of 2022 and 2023. The story also relies on the author's personal experience as a member of the Hope for Wildlife volunteer wildlife rescue team, and first-hand knowledge of the old house Hope used to operate out of, the annual Open House extravaganza, watching the wildlife rescue change and grow over time, and caring for injured wildlife herself. The author also knew Gretel the pine marten and Reid Patterson. *She is Hope for Wildlife* also incorporates information from social media sources and the 2011 book *Hope for Wildlife* by Ray MacLeod.

About Hope for Wildlife

Hope Swinimer and Gretel.

Since 1997, Hope for Wildlife has rehabilitated and released over 80,000 injured and orphaned wild animals representing over 250 species. It also provides educational outreach to schools, trains interns and engages a large team of volunteers, and is open for tours year-round. Animals treated at the wildlife rescue receive food, medicine, veterinarian care, shelter, and whatever else is needed to reduce suffering and, ideally, to ensure their successful return to the wild.

Hope for Wildlife relies on grants and donations to run the wildlife rehabilitation centre. To learn more about Hope for Wildlife or to donate to support Hope's work, and her dream, please visit hopeforwildlife.net.

About the Author & Illustrator

CALLEN SINGER PHOTO

Wanda Baxter lives on an old farm in Lunenburg County, Nova Scotia, with her long-time partner, Randy, their gregarious cat, George, and an ever-changing assortment of wildlife. Wanda has Masters degrees in English (with Creative Writing) and Environmental Design, and works as an environmental consultant primarily for non-profit environmental organizations. She is a volunteer on the dispatch team for Hope for Wildlife and is the author of *If I Had an Old House on the East Coast*, illustrated by Kat Frick Miller. This is her first book for children.

DAVID MACLEOD PHOTO

Leah Boudreau is a self-taught illustrator from Cape Breton Island. Her colourful and whimsical illustrations are often inspired by her life on the East Coast. Leah aspires to illustrate stories that will encourage kids to step outside and explore the world and all its little wonders. When Leah is not illustrating she can be found hiking with her dog, baking, reading, or simply curled up with a cozy cup of tea.